The First Year

by Christian Downey
illustrated by Tom McNeely

Editorial Offices: Glenview, Illinois • Parsippany, New Jersey • New York, New York
Sales Offices: Needham, Massachusetts • Duluth, Georgia • Glenview, Illinois
Coppell, Texas • Ontario, California • Mesa, Arizona

Every effort has been made to secure permission and provide appropriate credit for photographic material. The publisher deeply regrets any omission and pledges to correct errors called to its attention in subsequent editions.

Unless otherwise acknowledged, all photographs are the property of Scott Foresman, a division of Pearson Education.

Photo locators denoted as follows: Top (T), Center (C), Bottom (B), Left (L), Right (R), Background (Bkgd)

Opener: Illustrations by Tom McNeely

Photographs 16 ©DK Images

ISBN: 0-328-13359-0

4 5 6 7 8 9 10 V0G1 14 13 12 11 10 09 08 07 06

Chapter One

Jacob and Sarah arrived in Virginia with their parents in the early spring of 1630. They came on a large ship with many other families. The new land would be their home. Along with the others, they hoped to build a colony. It was a big change for them. Jacob and Sarah liked the open land. They wanted to explore and see new things.

First they had to build. Jacob and Sarah's father helped build barns and cabins.

"Father, can we help too?" asked Jacob.

"Yes, Father. What can we do?" asked Sarah.

"You can help find logs. Look in the forest for trees and fallen logs. We can make houses and boats out of them," said their father.

"Let's go, Sarah!" said Jacob.

Jacob and Sarah walked to the nearby woods.

Jacob and Sarah found many big trees and fallen logs. Their father and a few other men used them to build a new boat.

It was still early spring, so the weather was still cold. To help keep them warm, Jacob and Sarah's father made fires from the logs.

Jacob and Sarah's father also used the wood to make a gift. He sliced the wood thin, like paper, and sewed together the pages to make notepads. Father made one notepad for Jacob and another for Sarah.

Chapter Two

Spring came. The weather got warm and the ground thawed. Dew sparkled on the grass outside in the mornings. Jacob and Sarah's mother planted flowers in a garden next to their small house.

Jacob and Sarah liked to help their mother in the garden. Sarah helped put the seeds in the ground. Jacob watered them.

One day, their mother called them outside. "Sarah! Jacob! Come look!" she said.

The seeds that Sarah and Jacob had planted were now budding into flowers.

"It's growing! We did it!" said Jacob.

"Let's plant more!" said Sarah.

All through the spring, Sarah and Jacob helped their mother plant more flowers. Soon, the garden was blooming with every color!

The weather got much warmer as summer got closer. Fireflies came out at night to flutter all around the houses. Soon, the settlers were able to grow vegetables to eat. Native Americans who lived nearby showed them how. The settlers planted seeds to grow corn, squash, beans, and other crops. Jacob and Sarah liked to check on the vegetables.

Chapter Three

The settlers gave the Native Americans tools for cooking. They traded items. The settlers and the Native Americans each had things that could help the other. Jacob and Sarah were thankful. They liked the vegetables that the Native Americans helped them plant.

It had been raining for several days. Now that it was summer, the rain was warm. Jacob and Sarah did not like the many days of rain. They had to stay inside when the rains came.

Sarah and Jacob looked out the window at the patch of land where their garden grew.

"Jacob, when will the rain end?" asked Sarah.

"Soon, I hope. But at least the berries will grow!" said Jacob.

Their mother was growing blueberries and strawberries. She would make pies when they were ready.

Summer came and went. Soon it was early fall. The nights started getting colder again. When the frost came, the settlers tried to protect the crops and land.

To help predict what kind of weather might be coming, Jacob and Sarah's father had made a weather vane out of wood. He had cut the wood carefully with the blade of a knife.

Jacob and Sarah's father had placed the weather vane on top of the barn. It told them which way the wind blew. Jacob and Sarah loved to watch the weather vane twist and turn in the wind. They wanted to have their own!

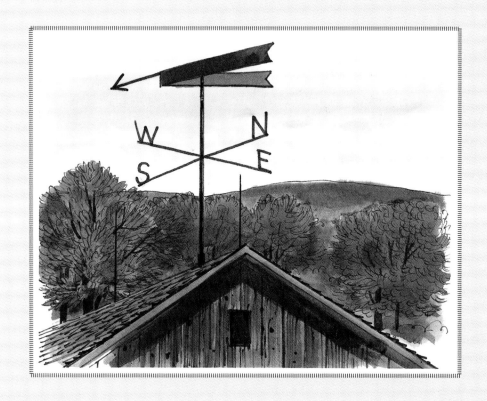

Chapter Four

In order to make their own weather vane, Jacob and Sarah first found a piece of rope. They hung the rope over the branch of a small tree that grew in their mother's garden. Then they tied a pointed piece of wood to the end of the rope. When the weather was good, they marked places in the dirt to show which way their weather vane pointed.

One rainy and windy day, they went out to the garden. "Sarah, which way is the wood pointing?" asked Jacob.

"It's pointing to the right," Sarah said.

"Which way did it point last night before the rain came?" asked Jacob.

"Last night it pointed to the left," said Sarah.

"So when it points left, rain might be coming!" said Jacob.

They ran home to tell their father. He would be happy that they helped.

Chapter Five

Jacob and Sarah had been working hard. They'd been working too hard to notice that fall was almost over! Winter was now not far off. One day, Jacob and Sarah's mother woke them early.

"Jacob! Sarah! Wake up! Today is the feast!" she said.

The settlers had been in Virginia for three full seasons. To celebrate, they decided to have a big feast. Jacob and Sarah helped their mother make a cake. When the cake was done, they cooled it on the windowsill. They walked to the big barn with their parents.

All of the settlers came to the feast. Their Native American friends came too. People brought bread, meat, cakes, and pics. They made everything themselves. Everyone shared. Jacob and Sarah ate the cake they made. When the feast ended, they went home to bed. Jacob and Sarah were thankful for their new home.

Edible Plants

Some birds and insects feed on the nectar found in plants and flowers. People also rely on plants for nourishment.

Not all plants and flowers are safe to eat. Some can be eaten raw, and others must be cooked. Some plants get sprayed with unsafe chemicals. Others may have dangerous growths.

Experts know how to identify wild or dangerous plants. They stay away from plants that are bitter and those with spines or thorns. It is safe to eat plants that blossom into food, such as strawberries, pumpkins, and tomatoes.

Certain plants, like mistletoe, are not safe to eat. Other plants, like ripe tomatoes on a vine, provide food for people.